what outlives us

what outlives us

poems by Larry Levy

atmosphere press

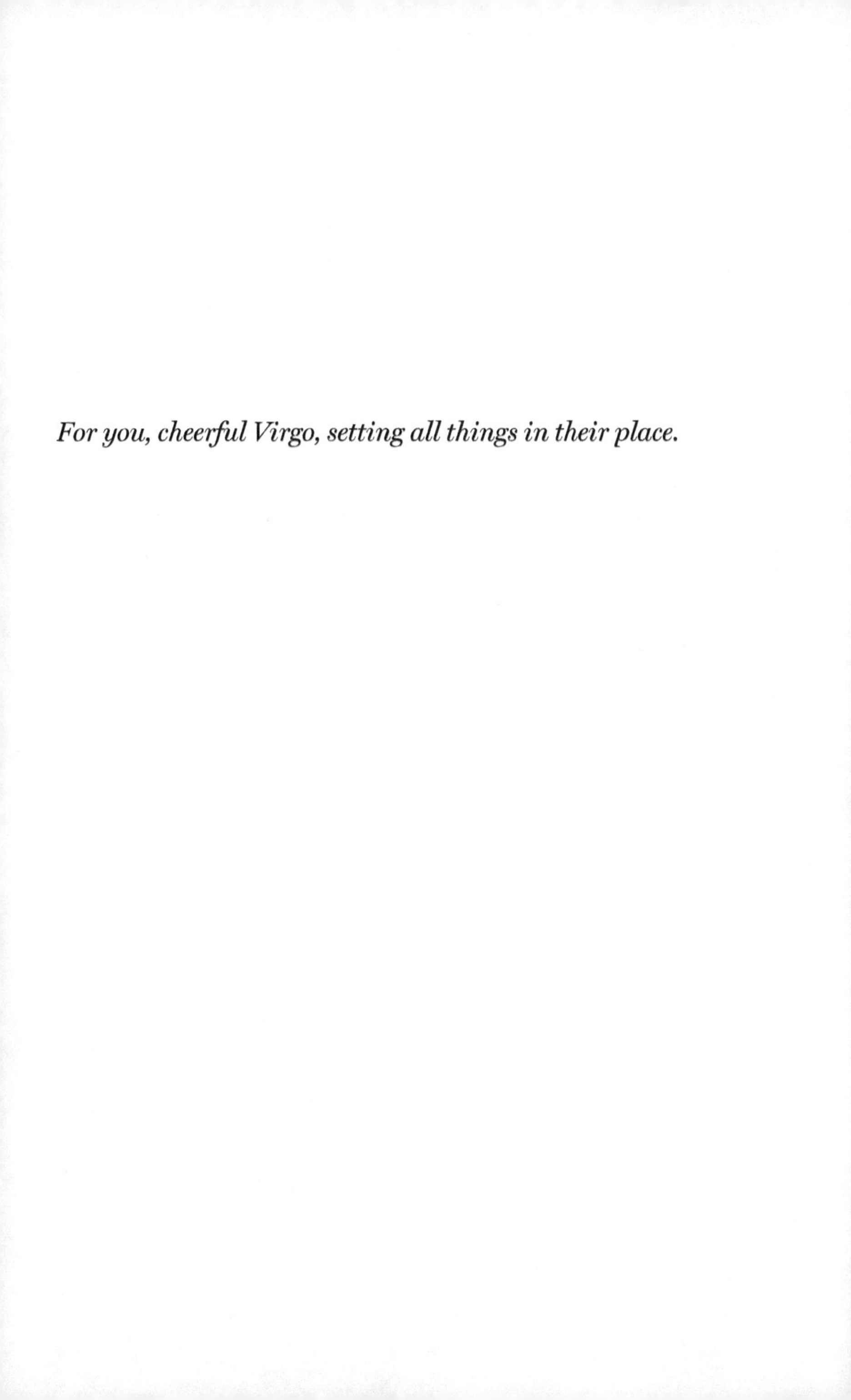

For you, cheerful Virgo, setting all things in their place.

Contents

III.   *Dressing The Wound*

A poem begins as...
a sense of wrong, a homesickness, a lovesickness.

~ Robert Frost

My poems are soft green.
My poems are also flaming crimson...

Mi verso es de un verde claro, y de un carmín encendido...

~ Pete Seeger (from José Martí)

I.   The Strong Throw Home

Yucatan

1.   *Language School*

In the company of native speakers
all seem to lose their voices.

Slowly the older boy opens up,
the others deferring to him.

How are you today, Teacher asks.
I am perfectamente, thank you.

My name is Juan Carlos,
but please call me García Bernal.

The younger boys laugh, the girls
rolling their eyes. Oh, he is suave.

To my right a young lady turns,
eyes downcast. I am Cynthia,

a little shy, nervous with strangers.
Oh, she is shy, Bernal says,

but we all see her. Like a hummingbird,
another boy's eyes dart at Cynthia.

She says, You are the first North American
I have ever spoken to.

2.   *Justina's World*

Our guide arrives this morning at six,
driving to places we cannot pronounce.

He stops at a hovel, door made of sticks,
an oval under graying palm thatch.

A henequen hammock hangs wall to wall.
Two pots and a pan hang from a beam.

*It isn't much, but this is all
her own,* he says. *This is home*

*for sixty years. Why move to the city?
She has chickens, almond trees,*

*well water. Who needs electricity
to wrap pavo in hoja de maíz,*

to grow chaya? Her body a crescent,
face open and wrinkled like the moon,

she takes my hand. She smells of mint,
offering an embrace. *I am not alone,*

she says. *My daughter comes by,
and my rooster sings to me at dawn.*

*In dreams, Enrique appears. It is he,
home again, and we lie down.*

3.   *The Ruins At Uxmal*

In a film at Museo Chocolate
a campesino slices football-size pods—
roasting beans—food for the gods,
the tourista's mocha latte.

Kings in this neighborhood
preferred the barista—a priest—
to pierce a volunteer's breast
for a vente cacao and blood.

Now everyone's heavenly home,
Starbucks or Caribou,
steams flavors like tiramisu
topped with an altar of foam.

4.   *Ex-Pat*

From the colony voted Best in the World,
she arrived at breakfast, hair tightly curled,

and hablas español with local spice,
venturing into past tense once or twice.

Though stuck in present, we understood
her rolling r's, subjunctive mood,

each noun's correct gender, never a wrong
south of the Rio Grande diphthong.

But when the cook, smiling *campesino*—
breakfast alive with *cilantro, cumino*—

offered that morning's creamy *frijoles,*
tortillas, huevos, red and green *moles,*

she muttered neither *gracias* nor *por favor,*
just *black coffee, Juan,* then out the door.

Juan has his passions, especially history—
not the good or the bad but the truth of it,
the stuff some legislators at home fear
will bring down America.

So this early morning he drives us
to the Municipal Cemetery.
Not exactly Chitzen-Itza's evening
sound and light show attracting

glowing newlyweds from the cruise ships.
Here acres of tombs speak, some ruined,
nameless; some newly chisled,
blinding under the Yucatecan sun.

One is pure, elegant marble,
a colonial, kneeling over a muerto,
the shroud's folds, seeming more cloth
than stone, her face leaning in lament.

A family tomb, Juan explains,
a family wealthy from hennequin,
the subservience of the indigenous,
the priests taking confessions

from them, newly baptized,
sharing their whispered anger
with the Governor's officers,
the consequences swift, severe.

Juan also shows us the memorial
to a champion of the Mayan pueblos,
hanged with his brothers. No saint,
he says. A young, American reporter

shared his commitments and bed.
She, invisible in history lessons.
Her stone adorned with glyphs,
leaning like Guadalupe's head

as if to better hear what
doves overhead are singing
about the world of today,
where a crusader like Juan

speaks without whispering,
without fearing retribution,
without his handsome, chiseled head
displayed nameless on a stake.

5.   *El Jardin de las Delicias*
          (The Garden of Earthly Delights)

Antonio burst from the compound gate,
shirtless, big bellied, his Catalan Spanish
all staccato and fortissimo.

I caught maybe every tenth word,
but he was clearly *muy vivo*
like a bull let loose into the arena

ready to begin the show.
Our friend Juan embraced him,
his own voice amplifying,

picking up speed and profanities.
Such was Antonio's effect on everyone.
He was the host, comfortable in his flesh

and appetites. He threw fistfuls
of *cebollas* on a grill, stoking the fire
with wads of dried grass, smoke and flames

whooshing upward, blackening the bulbs.
Overwhelmed, I stepped back from the wave
of heat to meet his other guests

seated around a large cement table
under the *mamey* trees. Including our friend,
there were three Juans, Margarita, William,

Ingrid, Gaby, Neo, Ali, Cher, and myself.
In addition to various dialects of Spanish,
the talk erupted in English, German,

combinations of all three, and also Polish.
Some sentences began in one language
and ended in another. Sometimes one speaker

held the floor. More often several
spoke at once. Seldom did anyone speak
without another's aside, footnote,

embellishment, minority report, guffaw,
or plea from the prosecution or defense.
Occasionally someone broke into song.

The *cebollas* arrived, smacked onto the table,
well-charred, peeled, and dipped in almond purée.
With the flow of wine and rum and *cerveza*

voices flowed like some kind of fugue,
entrances, exits, impromptu, nearly incoherent.
After four glasses of *blanco*, Cher's Spanish

grew fearless, and Juan from Malaga told jokes
about Pepita and a large penis,
and trilingual Juan translated the Spanish word

for *asshole*, the Mayan for *motherfucker,*
and we all sliced off hunks of grilled beef,
more than I'd eaten in six months,

and even vegetarian Ali, who told me
she was *a natural girl,* nibbled red chorizo
with sweet red wine, and for twenty minutes

Antonio tried to explain the origin of *Texas*
and *Miami* and *Colorado* and especially *California,*
something about *un libro* and *un paradiso,*

but we never learned the book's title
nor much of anything else from him
except how much pleasure everyone took

in contributing chapters to the story,
extending it into a divine comedy, until
the compound's owner came down

from her bedroom, padding through the dark
in her housecoat and slippers, speaking softly
and with obvious courtesy to Antonio

about the guards trying to sleep upstairs
after their long day, and Antonio sort of listening,
still bellowing, and eventually getting her to join us,

and then her husband, too, and then two Chihuahuas
little bigger than rats skittering under the table
for scraps of *arrachera* steak or *nopalitos*,

and one slim *gato*, a bell around its neck,
which Ali fed slices of salami, while William
drank his tall glasses of clamato into which

he drizzled a homemade habanero salsa
from a jar, telling me of his love for the Yankees
and Derek Jeter, and his three sons who played

first base and centerfield and he, an old right fielder,
able in his youth to make the strong throw home,
and he and everyone clicking on handhelds,

sharing snapshots of grandchildren
and of themselves from back in the day when they
were beautiful with thick hair and smooth faces,

and Ali recalling her father in his last days
forgiving her for leaving the Church and sharing
a bed before marriage with multilingual Juan,

and Ingrid telling of her four husbands, three dead,
and Margarita nicknaming her *the Black Widow*—
and all had such tales, old and new and partly true.

Down South

The barista curls around a word,
adding a syllable and then a third.

I am not sure what I just heard.

She finds my accent somewhat alien.
Am I from England or Canadian?

She smiles warmly, profoundly cheerful.
I delight in her molasses earful.

We creatures from a world apart,
she, red clay born; my Yankee heart—

grandparents Eastern European—
is not remotely Tennessean.

She serves me in a china cup.
I leave her a one-dollar tip.

In County Clare

Will it rain? I ask her, Belfast-born.
Oh, you'll get wet for sure.
So into a water-tight trunk
I pack waterproof gear
she says I'll need *oh, everywhere.*
Now a veil of weather drips
off my cap's soggy bill,
blurring my Burrens map.
I climb a spongy path
to a green bluff above a bay.
Below a farmer and son plow
perfect furrows, planting hay,
a hard day to do good work.
Oh, the world's under a damp cloud
after news that Heaney's gone.
*Tell me what's the good word,
Friend?* I wonder, hiking ridges
all the way down. We once met
and will again within his pages.
Today it rained and I got wet
I write in my journal.
The world over, others note
his honors, compare him to Yeats.
Rain soaks my impermeable coat
until, overflowing, I recite lines
I will not, cannot forget.
*Today the West was green with mist
and all of Ireland was wet.*

Friday Evening in Jerusalem

The heat is quenched. The air cools.
A breeze wafts over gritty hills.

Pale under the workaday sun, stones
glow blue-green beneath the moon.

Traffic slows, all but disappears.
Shopkeepers shutter windows and doors.

Three stars in the bottomless sky
silence disputations with a sigh.

Small birds grow silent in the trees.
Believers, as commanded, rise—

the poor, innocent, weary, undone—
chanting *God is great! The Lord is One.*

On Ben Yehuda near Jaffa Road,
families stroll. Then the bombs explode.

Memorial Day

In the 1950's, neighborhood kids
bivouacked, counting off by twos,
determining foes and friendly sides.
No volunteers. No one could choose
to be cowboys, blue coats or reds,
Krauts, Japs, or Kickapoos.

We skulked under bushes, lay by a fence,
evening shadows our closest friend.
Our aim, our purpose, to pounce,
fire first, hollering *Got you! You're dead!*
From out of the silence to announce
I got Chuck. I got Andy. I got Ed.

My brothers. But if one was Custer
another was Cochise or Black Elk.
If one was Hirohito or Hitler,
another was Murphy or Sergeant York.
Once I was the Duke and he Quanah Parker,
disappearing on horseback into the dark.

A neighbor, cousin, someone
quick—but occasionally too slow
for enemies we could not outrun.
Where lie those children now?
Faceless under the desert sun?
Nameless in the Afghan snow?

Yearbook, Fifty Years Later

Darkness knows my secrets read his grind.
After commencement he joined the Corps.
One moonless night within the year
while walking point he tripped a wire.
They flew home all that they could find.

A lifetime later, she hears his name
resurrected over tea with friends.
Goodness, she says, but who's to blame?
His buddies enlisted to defend,
believed they heard a Higher Call.

Maybe she passed him in the hall
nodding, maybe not even that.
She brainstorms to recall
if they'd shared a class, where he sat,
who shared his table during lunch.

The best she manages is a hunch:
Did he take German? Build a car?
Sit in on trombone in a pinch?
She recalls his going off to War,
his dark eyes, dark hair.

Once By the Atlantic

1.   On Tybee Island

If I cannot see heaven from here,
for now I'll take this sweep of shore,

the miles of sand, tide so far out
my soul has no trace of doubt.

For now the memory of words,
the silence of weightless birds

broken by their electric call
is plenty for me, maybe all

I need, a damp breeze in my face.
If not heaven, still a pleasant place

to walk beyond the lighthouse, then
trace my footprints home again.

2.   *Seal*

While I walk damp sand
in the mute sunrise,

she stares just off land
with long-lashed eyes,

bobbing, an inflatable toy
in the Atlantic waves,

shuttering her whiskered nose,
which is how she survives.

She dives through a school
swirled in a mass,

swallowing whole
a dozen in a pass.

Sleepy-eyed, sated then,
at leisure like a log,

she assumes mammalian Zen,
almost smiling, like a dog,

facing into the offshore wind,
oblivious to humankind.

3.   *Stones*

At dawn they step down to the shore,
walking where the smooth stones are.

She finds a pebble, unblemished as the pearl
looped around her neck as a girl.

His rock, green as the waves,
preserves flora from ancient graves.

The sun illuminates the bluff,
her face furrowing in a laugh.

He goes bare-toed
in the mud, the out-going tide.

Her stone glinting, his with a leaf—
one for remembrance, one for long life.

For miles, in silence, they inhale the wind.
Returning, she says *Oh, this is good!*

4.   *This Part of the World*

The pines glow in the twilight sun.
A last golf cart glides down a lane
past a still pond, a stiller crane,
past a silhouetted couple on a late run,
a widow game on a borrowed knee,
all within the briny smell of the bay.

Bridge partners hit the early buffet
for all the comfort they can put away
for $9.99. In many a kitchenette
blenders churn beverages salty and tart
to sip while lounging on the lanai.
And small, dark men sweep the street—

the streets manicured with Spanish names
like *Bella Vida, Duerma Bien.*
They smile back when smiled upon,
their speech flowing with vowels and rhymes,
r's rolling like surf beneath palms,
the palms shedding their wrinkled skin.

How soon and quickly the lights go out
on this part of the world! How complete
the dark on the dock and boat!
I lie awake, taking in the quiet, sweet
smile of the moon, then drift
into night under my cool sheet.

II. Story Problems

My Brilliant Career

Stubby as a Bassett,
I belted one off the gym wall,
another over Barbados' fence,
ripping stitches on our only ball.

In the playground rag-tag guys
tossed the bat to choose first-ups.
Our baselines sandy as Charlotte beach,
we settled scores, yelping like pups.

In the League, Coach's son pitched.
Parents barked their kid's mistakes.
My flannels squeezed my ripe belly.
My hands hummed with the shakes.

I muffed a roller, whiffed at bat,
then hit one like the Fourth of July,
a cherry bomb, a Roman candle,
a rocket splitting the outfield sky.

I chugged the bases, grinning
at slip-ups and sudden success.
Sugar Kings cap and shirttail flying,
double-knot laces flapping loose,

I slid home to a thousand cheers.
Dad missed that game because
of work, but at supper, filling him in,
I felt like the hero I was.

Dented Schwinn

I wanted a bicycle, but not the kind
without gears, or with gears that grind.
My dad called this gem *a real find,*

what salespeople now call *gently used.*
He encouraged me to be enthused,
take her for a spin. Suddenly I found

myself skidding, face to the ground,
nearly concussed, confused
that he thought this junker the kind

his second child could glide around,
cruising the streets and fields, amused
and enlightened by what I might find—

winding paths to pedal, to unwind;
mysteries that occasionally bruised
me into thought, not the easy kind.

I See the Summer Children

I dove for the tennis ball Dad tossed
out of reach, always just out of reach.

And built canals and castles on the beach
which after lunch were quickly lost

to larger waves, the trickle of tide.
And longed to be a little more

finned like fish, shining like the shore.
And dozed on the homeward ride

wishing the time were less brief—
swimming to the last barrel and past—

Ontario—cool, green, wrinkled, vast,
thick with seaweed, dying alewife.

Dad cradled me sleeping up the stairs,
the lake damp in my bleached hair.

Kindergarten

My hair was cut short, white at the temples
after a summer of afternoons at the beach.
Mom aimed her Brownie while I stood
next to Eddie, taller than I could reach.

He took my hand as we crossed Clinton
at the yellow lines, the safety patrol boys
holding back cars. They seemed so large,
the fifth graders, and my green eyes,

too, as we entered the school, its dark,
warm hallways, and finally my room
with posters I could partly read,
and there was a table with my name,

a place for me to color and count.
At noon I showed what I had made,
a drawing of Miss B with teeth.
She whispered not to be afraid.

Mascot

Behind Portanova's house
the field waved chest-high
with thorns and burrs,
our Hamburger Hill during
mid-summer's wars.

Mogavero's gang raked
the weeds below, pitching
hardball clods
of clay onto our platoon,
our neighborhood.

Andy galloped the flank.
Chuck geronimo-ed ahead.
Eddie pitched grenades
of uprooted goldenrod,
mouthing shell-burst sounds.

I was still in short pants,
the kid others boosted
over the barbed fence.
They said I was too young
to take a chance.

Elephant

Kids crowded near Sally's cage,
eyes wide at her watery eyes
and wrinkled skin. Her large ears
overflowed with their *ahhs.*

her trunk stretching across
the moat, a delicate hand
grasping a grape or apple slice.
Some days she seemed to stand

still as a statue, a constant
when we were young, our small
legs rambling the zoo, her leg
straining a chain fixed to the wall.

Eighth Grade Dialogues

He explained his bald spot was hereditary,
so I asked if my dad was bald would I also lose my hair?
Not necessarily he replied.
If it rained every July 4th for ten years
would it rain this coming July 4th?
Not necessarily.
If I earned a 'B' on the first five marking periods
would I most likely earn a 'B' in the sixth?
Not necessarily. Study better and see.
But what if we tossed ten apples
in the air and they all came down,
would the 11th tossed apple also fall?
Most likely. But don't take my word.
So I heaved ball after ball to the gym rafters,
every one, I reported back, descending.
If all men die he asked,
and if Socrates is a man,
will he also die?
After I left junior high,
Mr. Disinger disappeared from my life.
Why did I never go back to see him?
If most eighth graders live unexamined lives,
and if I was a typical eighth grader, then most likely
I did not reflect on my teacher's significance.
Most likely I did not consider myself mortal either,
nor think about my teacher's mortality, nor Socrates'
too, too solid flesh, melting, dissolving into a dew.

Beautiful Game

Coach preached to fake left,
drive right off the left foot, lay
the ball right-handed, deft
off the board. *The right way*

he repeated: Off right foot. Up left hand.
But nights, under the porch light
or on the Y hardwood, we heard
an inner voice—levitate,

fly to the rim, give and go,
pick and roll, pop from the key,
no look feed, breakneck flow,
five-part cacophony.

Next day, Coach silenced the noise:
Play the right way. My way, boys.

Sophomore Year

The room is dark as the Twelfth of Never.
I cannot tell my hat from my glove.
Other guys, glassy-eyed and clever,
embrace their dates, gaga with love.

It feels like love, this cheeky sweat,
trembling arms embracing a waist,
hair lathered like appaloosas in heat,
everyone ripening and red-faced.

On the phonograph, a pile of LPs
plop on one another—a crooner
adoring every woman he sees.
Johnny Mathis will *Make Me Yours*.

In the electric oven, rustle of cloth,
clink of belt buckle, whirr of zipper.
In another corner, sharp intake of breath—
the older kids, cooler, hipper.

My date breaks things off,
nudges me with her moist hands.
When I lean in, she stifles a cough,
whispering *Can't we just be friends?*

Yearbook

Someone transparent, incomplete—
did she live on a dead-end street?

Her bird's nest hair, raccoon eyes—
did she hang out with theater guys?

I cannot recall a word she said—
Or maybe I misunderstood

her mismatched socks,
paint-spattered smocks.

Did anyone ever take her hand?
Did she once earn a reprimand

for her million mile stare
out the window toward who knows where?

I've forgotten a lot, except her look
when we signed each other's book.

Fraternity Rush

First week at school I accepted a bid,
brothers embracing me with a song,
sharing the secret grip. *Way to go, Kid*,
the President winked. It didn't last long.

Soon, the Pledge Master, hefty and tall,
screamed, spitting, as if I were deaf,
to *give me fifty*. I rolled an eyeball—
then *sixty more*. It was never enough.

Early Saturdays I mopped the floor,
scrubbed sinks, scoured toilet bowls.
At midnight, pounding on my door,
they shouted *you don't have the balls*.

Half-asleep, half-dressed in line,
I got reamed for missing a spot—
Stupid Pledge! Where is your brain?
I wondered the same. I wondered a lot,

especially when they ridiculed others
who did not look or think like them,
when they proclaimed *all men are brothers*
while dinging him and him and him.

Why did I stick it out, swear an oath
with many words I had no faith in?
I knew in my core, in every breath,
they were not—would never be—my kin.

Conference with My Teacher

I recall her home, carpeted and dark,
the absence of a television,
a lamp shadowing walls of books.
Her raised eyebrow suggested an addition,

or subtraction she preferred.
Sometimes, eyes amused and wide,
her finger tapped a single word.
That's good, she said. That's good.

She served tea, a slice of cake.
She was nearing retirement age,
but I recall how softly she spoke
while studying my page.

The Workshop

They correct me quickly when I say
they are fourth graders. Oh pardon—fifth!
Certainly they are eleven, soon to be twelve.

What does one need to write poetry?
And many arms stretch out
of their eleven-year-old sockets.

Paper they shout. *A pencil!*
Or a pen one blurts. *A writing tool!*
And then, going abstract—*imagination!*

A Brain! A Heart! The Nerve I want to add,
when one worried soul calls out
Something to Write About!

Ah, and here comes lesson one:
As Rilke wrote the young poet,
Even if you were locked away in prison

faced with brick walls only, maybe
only a small, high, barred window of sky,
even then, they could not take away

your childhood. They are quiet now,
studying me, decades removed from
the New World explorers, being cut

from the team, culled from the herd,
the story problems, the clarinet keys,
the entrances and exits of the heart,

the pulse in my pen, the fire and ice
when I wrote her that note that made
us both go red in the face.

Honor Student

When Rebecca read her poem
to the class, her hair reflected
fluorescent light like the model's hair

in the shampoo advertisements,
and like the cool cathode tube,
her voice flickered, faint, fainter,

then hardly there. I wished her words
might cling like a spider's filament,
dwell in a more local habitation—

a doorway, a maple leaf,
a real toad—call us to things
of this world for love's sake.

What brands you with a tongue of fire?
What burns your heart until you ache?

Dougie

I see him barreling down the wing,
face glowing, ball firmly at his feet.
The opposing back stumbles to meet
his charge, but Doug brakes, retreats
as if the ball, fastened on a string,
knew his mind, his fierce will—
then blasts it into the upper goal.

And I recall a game three quarters in—
how more than once he had a shot
then suddenly seemed to forget
where his feet were, their sweet spot,
and sent it way wide off his shin.
It was as if he'd lost his touch
or, fists balled, wanted it too much.

Coach Vince

In practices back then we kneeled
in a playground around a map,
a bird's-eye view of a soccer field.

Our players, under nine years old,
learned to pass, move to space, to trap—
to mark opponents without being told,

when open in the box to fire away,
to share orange slices, to clap
for everyone who came to play.

On Saturdays fifteen fidgety boys,
one girl, all itching for a scrap,
stampeded between goals, making noise.

We won mostly, more often than not.
When we lost, Vince, full of hope,
smiled, the best lesson he taught.

Her Students

Although it will take
more than five years,
she will graduate to thousands
of dollars in debt
with a license to teach seventh graders,
thousands of them, some mute,
some with no volume control,

who come in many sizes and fabrics
like marked down clothes at Goodwill
hung too closely together
so that they are hard to reach,
get tangled, fall in a heap on the floor,
mislabeled, missing a button,
stained on the sleeve, knee

ripped, a hole over the heart.
She will give them air, space,
smooth their wrinkles—
no steam, no high heat—by hand.
She will open windows,
take care their big box Crayolas
neither run nor fade.

To a Shy Student

I am pleased to be your Facebook,
your virtual friend. We used to see one another
Tuesday mornings, face-to-face.

You did not actually
look me in the eye, but sideways, suspicious
of me, college, and your place.

What were you, barely seventeen?
And the other Hannah was so chatty,
full of quips and confidence,

while you remained
silent for weeks, but not wordless, slipping me
your pages, the pages in a wry voice,

so indirect and wiry.
In your writing I could almost see
a smile. I thought—no, I was sure—

there was a smile. There it is now
in your Facebook photos,
your young face, knowing and pure.

Gladly Teach

In yearbook shots her waistline spreads,
glasses thicken, hair disappears.
Biography first, argument next—
the semester schedule fixed for years,

decades describing a career.
Teaching high school is complex
she sighs over donuts and midday meds,
thumbs tapping text after text.

What reward did you expect?
a colleague asks. *The Book of Kells?*
His pen bloodies what's incorrect,
her will bowing to the bells.

Down you go to special hells
he jokes, briefcase overflowing with doubt.
But it's Friday, and paychecks pay the bills.
She hums a dirge while clocking out,

visits the Home to check on Mother,
then four blocks to her three room flat.
She scrolls through one screen or another,
fixes dinner for one, one for the cat.

Then closes a window, draws the shade.
Finding her chapter she is soon deep
in a world Barbara Cartland made,
a Pirate King sailing into her sleep.

The Absent Professor

Lecturing, he lost his place.
Something about a political theory.
He had a distance in his face,
blinking, straightening his tie.

He was not at all sure where
his thread or theme had gone.
A moment ago it was right there.
His students, silent, heads down,

pretended they were not confused.
Finally, gathering papers and books,
he told everyone they were excused,
returning to his office. But it wasn't his.

Word got around he seemed OK—
the tilt of his head, bemused eyes,
slight smile, a joke served dry,
a well-timed word to the wise

in a meeting, the hall, most days
in his overflowing classes.
Once he misplaced his keys,
and for a few days his glasses,

but he was so often deep in thought
friends assumed it was ordinary stuff.
Then, without his shoes or coat,
one winter day he wandered off.

What Do People Do All Day?

Every night as he dozed in bed
my son turned the cartoon pages
of Richard Scarry's book showing
what the fireman did, the jet pilot,
the livestock farmer, the sea captain—
each page a way to count one's days.

He dreamed, so he said later,
of growing up, plowing, soaring,
rescuing cats and children in distress.
In real life he could not pass
a steam shovel, a fire station,
a corral, or better, a meadow of ponies.

He pitched his fantasies to me
until my knees ached. He foresaw
inventions like Leonardo's, lighter
than air. He painted birds
from God's world in primary colors.
He kicked and chattered in his sleep.

Now, midnights, he squints
through a lens, alone in the dark,
charting life in miniature. His sedan
is in the shop with undiagnosed
discontents. He wants to invest
in a newer car with more libido.

He imagines turning the page
to other versions of this life.
He imagines getting and spending
with larger numbers. He dreams
of wind in his face on a Western slope,
tacking as his telltale snaps to a westerly.

My Daughter's Dress

This morning, rushing to work,
she thinks dressmakers assume
every woman has longer arms
or a helping hand in the room.

Her reach falls short of the clasp.
She slept funny, alone in her bed.
Her cats, lacking thumbs,
brush her legs instead.

She hopes for a crosstown guest
on the El who doesn't mind
a stranger's shy request.
Far away, I hope someone kind

provides no less than I—
and fastens her hook and eye.

Recipe

This morning you're shopping for fish,
the market offering perch and pike.
We'll fix the wine and caper dish
you know I like.

Of course, you like it just as much
with mushrooms, cannellini beans,
lemon juice, your piquant touch
with wilted greens.

You like sticking to the book
but tolerate my sorcerer's brew.
Yet side-by-side we cook
a savory stew

with warm and broken bread,
the sweet and pungent marinade
of our days, of what we've said,
and what we've made.

Dinner with Friends

Skip downed a three-olive martini.
Julia refreshed her chardonnay.
Larry took a whack at Mussolini.
Cheryl's dish and spoon ran away.

Cheryl's cow jumped over the moon.
Vegetarian Skip ate kidney pie.
Julia went aerobic from dawn to noon.
Larry ranted over whiskey and rye.

Larry shot every arrow in his quiver.
Once upon a time Cheryl came late.
Skipper waded across the river.
Elegant Julia licked her plate.

Julia thumbed her last gob of gravy.
Larry forgot his long-sleeved coat.
Cheryl's daddy joined the Navy.
And Skip, famished, ate the goat.

To You

When you were a kid—
dark eyes smirking,
high diving on the bed—
was I already lurking
in your heart and head?

Were we already paired—
my secret self
to a dream you—declared
in sickness and in health?
Would we have dared

to hold hands, for heaven's sake?
Shared a balloon, a unicorn?
Now candles on your cake
give any room you're in a glow.
I am glad you were born

in September, cheerful Virgo,
setting all things in their place.
And I, your sometime hero,
adoring your adorable face
that saw our future years ago.

Going Home

I detour through the old neighborhood,
streets now somehow less wide.
Now sprinklers rainbow
over the weedless lawns,
maples a tunnel of shade.

Gone, the goldenrod fields.
Gone, the playground diamonds.
The willow—a fire bush of birds.
Gardens lined with petunias
border childless yards.

Here, my brother, a late bloomer,
taught irregular kids to conform.
My sister, stars lining her wall,
aged steadily bitter, silent
as the plum staked in a storm.

Here they lay down, kicking in their sleep.
I slept here, too, my bed a ship,
sails full on the stillest night,
my mind a full spectrum of dreams
of falling, wings straining in flight.

III.   Dressing the Wound

Our Daily Bread

1.　　　　*When America Was Great*

Each spring the fanboys came—
wealthy, smiling, pearly white—
celebrating the Gentleman's Game.

Azaleas, bursting and bright,
dogwood, crab, and holly—
April's fragile blooms—

welcomed them, hale and jolly,
in gated gardens and rooms
where they joked of traps and trees,

of Mark Twain's *spoiled walk,*
then hooked and sliced from tees
out-of-bounds from woman talk.

The Captains, the Oligarchs
were waited on, groomed.
Their caddies, invisible and dark,

as privilege assumed.

2.   *Thine is the Kingdom*

He stares into the lens,
interrupting without a blink,

insisting he alone comprehends
how his failing enemies stink.

They appear in various disguises,
accusations foul with fakery.

Before dawn his bread rises,
sustenance from his half-bakery.

Eyes flitting from maps to charts,
he supposes ruling is a cinch—

Master the Machiavellian arts.
Scowl for photos. Never flinch.

Never apologize.
Remind everyone your name

trumps others' alibis.
Always assign blame.

3.   *A Reporter's Reply*

We waited days after your abrasions
to ask about what should be obvious—
if not to you and your Caucasians
then anyway to most of us

whose storage is huge and volatile,
memory quickening with megabits,
who buy gigabytes by the barrel
and do not suffer hypocrites,

bullies, the bait and switcher.
We see your glitter is not gold,
your spun wool not one thread richer
than your bald lies often told.

We realize you're more than loud.
Toadies convolute what you stated,
insisting your pinpricks make them proud—
your enemies so *sad, so overrated.*

But we hear what you just said—
you, an Emperor the devil made.
If you speak truth, then truth is dead.
Oh, how you'd like us to be afraid!

4.   *You're Fired!*

When he won't look me in the eye
but insists that what he says is true,
what others say must be a lie.

Among his listeners a rare few
accept him at his every word.
Can't understand it, but some do,

no matter how cockeyed or absurd.
If *black is white,* if *night is day,*
it matters not what I just heard.

What matters is what serviles say,
stories altered by the hour,
falsehoods in the name of power.

Support! Or else I'm on my way—
subtracted, mentioned nevermore,
except with prefixes *sad!* or *poor!*

I cannot stay, cannot reply.
My name's unscrewed above the door,
slandering my deep heart's core.

5.   *Logos, Pathos, Ethos*

During the endless campaign this year,
voices shilling like tinnitus in my ear,
I drove to Mt. Pleasant, the narrow road.

A billboard rose every quarter mile,
one hawking used cars, the owner's smile
full of yard-high teeth. My giant friend!

One with a t-bone, an acre of beef
requiring a chainsaw instead of a knife.
Enough to feed my neighborhood.

And one calling for blood,
for nothing less than a firing squad.
Their candidate is wrong with God

proposed the camouflaged figure—
Vote for our finger on the trigger!

6.   *For My Foes And For My Friends*

Of all the sad things happening now,
every conversation a yea or nay,
perhaps few things are sadder than
men being wolves to man.

One hardly offers a single thought
before a neighbor takes a bite,
vigorously working jaws and snout
then swallowing or spitting out

all that is evident and mistaken,
criminally, irredeemably broken,
lacking decency and sense
from the Dawn of Time and since.

Should I exhale, perhaps rebut,
retreat, keep my pie hole shut?
Should I express a thing or two
when almost anything won't do,

won't accomplish what I feel,
or, most of all, begin to heal?

Letting Go

His eyes scan the room
like a wounded pup.
If he hears his name
he doesn't sit up

but shifts his leg.
His left arm rises,
bends as if to hug
unfamiliar faces.

We urge *Do it again*,
but he's gone, asleep
in a wilderness, alone.
From far, from deep,

a voice whispers *Hope*,
a voice something like my own.

Released on Waivers

Edgar Herbert Levy (1945-2016)

I am surprised by this honor
my brother spoke into the mic,
am pleased to join the Something Bears
and will give my best for their sake,

returning them to their winning ways.
A real bear sat next to Ed,
massive jaws open, sizing up
his curly, free-agent head.

The Coach cleared his throat:
Our organization welcomes Mr. Levy.
We know he will contribute
with his speed and veteran savvy.

It was a dream, of course.
Ed suffered apnea, bad knees,
a grizzly's hefty paunch,
diabetes. His best days

were behind him. But even
in the dream I knew he was gone.
Still, it made a dream sense,
even the bear. Maybe wishes begin

in dreams. Maybe in heaven
Ed recovered what years betrayed,
regaining his legs, his heart for sports,
even whatever sport these Bears played.

To A Former Runner

He used to run five miles at dawn,
later competing in 10 K's,
eventually the marathon,
and all of this on burning knees,

one that had been locked and cut.
The orthopedist advised he quit,
take up swimming or cycling, but
running was his strongest suit,

necessary and genuine.
He told himself the chronic hurt
would melt away a mile in,
the loping rhythm in his heart

persuading him he was immune
from time. But time spoke soon.

Spring Training

It's still sub-zero, but in the South
the hometown team, old and new faces,
stretch the same frost-bitten places,
hamstrings, quads, mostly the mouth,
to rag on each other's fading youth:
You're looking good—beefy, lame.
You still bringin' that pitiful game?

They love one another all the same—
boys tattooed, men turning gray,
accented from Goshen to Maracay,
everyone eager to make their name.
They run in circles, sliding home
to Compton, Tidewater, Puerto Rico,
Miami, Lafayette, Tampico.

And reporters wave familiar mics
at the Next Sure Thing, the grizzled Ace
who fires off clichés to clear some space.
And the Old Coach ponders what he likes—
knocking dirt clods from his spikes,
tiptoeing over the infield lime
drawling *we'll take 'er one day at a time.*

Interview with Sanchez

Cropped hair flecked with gray,
he slouches in the dugout corner,
slider fooling no one any longer—
I tell you, Amigo, back in the day
I often broke one down and away.

Under the unforgiving sun
he shrugs away past shoulder tears,
scars of many innings and years.
You writers believe I may be done,
but I remember when I began—

throwing strikes was easy, Man.
Catchers mitt—I hit it square,
batters often buckling in fear.
American scout says I have a gun.
Coach says my fastball's on fire.

Now, let's face it, not so much.
After the knife I still have pain.
My knees say the clouds bring rain.
But no soy muerto. I have the touch
and, better than before, the brain.

He rises. *I am not the kind who quits.*
His ankles click like castanets.

The Artist in her Studio

Her elders often spent their days
hoeing a row or felling trees,
reshaping nature as they pleased.
So it is her nature, so she says,

to prefer being outdoors to in,
tending begonias on rural knees
as if in prayer, avoiding the sin
(so her Mom said) of being at ease,

reclining where no afternoon sun
warms the back. She bows to dirt,
spading, watering, never done,
wiping cracked palms on her shirt.

An hour she wants me to believe.
An hour later she turns instead
to her saw, yanking it alive
to walk the yard, culling the dead.

Prayer for the Solstice

A wren startles early morning.
Cedars burst into cardinal song,
branches silhouetted in the dawn.
The day awakens slow and long.

Now our endless sky is burning.
The eastern flower plot explodes
in violet, yellow, shades of green.
The sun calls us from our beds.

Even the tall maples lean,
inhaling light, more light still.
Evening finally draws its curtain,
dimming toward the Fall.

In the dark we learn to trust
tomorrow, and are blessed.

Transported

After work Dad stopped at the library
on his way home, filling bags to the brim
with thrillers for himself, romances for Mom,
their covers promising wishes and shocks,
and for me codes and limericks.

I loved one adventure about
a meadow mouse and Billy Mink,
and one about a boy my age who broke
a mustang colt and learned to ride.
We all traveled beyond the neighborhood,

reading. We were like frigates bound
for New Worlds, a cargo of ropes,
barrels of rum, and scrolled maps
enough to see through the dark unknown,
to travel through time before we knew

where an evening or a decade went.
We returned heavy with ambergris,
sea-silver pearls, and Golden Fleece,
bright birds dozing in gilded cages—
and my parents dozing before pages

of stories that riddled without resolve
in languages no longer spoken,
the words like music, like water falling.
Oh, my father and mother! May you awaken
to your dreams, to a magical calling
of longing and belonging

Dressing the Wound

Gloved, they unwrapped her leg
bound thigh to ankle, unhooking the clasps
stretching and holding the bandage,
then removing the damp, shriveled gauze
from the valley of the wound,
the flesh raw, seeping, unapologetic.
While they tended, she lay on her back
asking how things went at work
and how each was feeling that evening,

as if they were the ones whose vein
had been harvested. He told
her about a co-worker, miserable
with clients and supervisors,
who was also making his days long.
A wounded person she said.
He soaked fresh cloth in saline,
packing gently in layers, filling
the excavation, wrapping the whole leg

around and around, not too tight,
letting it breathe. *Good to go?*
he asked? *Good as new* she replied.
After plumping her pillows,
they drew her up the bed,
all giggling that during the night
she would somehow inch her way down.
They kissed her good night,
dimming the lamp on their way out.

Not Even Past

When I turned twenty, my mother said
she had no more to teach me, and I agreed,
because I was young in the heart and head
and despite all my schooling could not read

her resolve when her parents left,
and dad collapsed, and her daughter
stopped speaking to her. I sift
through memories of her ready laughter,

her musical and wise Odessa Yiddish,
recalling the night of her operation
when she bantered with nurses, fed me fish
and fries, her final meal and lesson.

Or maybe not so final. She once said
when her regrets became too much
she went upstairs to her empty bed
pulling the covers over her head.

So maybe she continues to teach
a way to weather grief.
She smiled, unsteady on a crutch—
Better to limp than crawl through life.

Was she ever happy? I suppose
she steeled her heart against her fears.
Perhaps she learned to compose
her public face beyond tears.

For Father's Day

No stogies, no bourbon.
No fire-roasting, butter
beef, deep-dish,
flavor infusing
bacon piled on ribs.
No long driver, no
up-my-game DVD.

Nothing with dogs or ducks,
bullets or hip waders,
outboard or inboard.
No payload or long haul.
No cure for the common
weed. No beard edger,
comb over, or easy over

joint replacer. Am I not
hip enough? No tools,
no hardware. We can dig it
all by our lonesomes.
No gizmos. No handhelds
except yours in mine,
dear weathered, smiling face.

What Outlives Us

Cigar boxes stacked on his bench,
although he never chewed nor smoked.

Assorted bolts, a rusty wrench,
a chipped screwdriver he liked.

Here, his handy-dandy pliers
charred from testing a basement fuse

that sparked alive with electrical fires
and red-hot words he'd rarely use.

Stashes of chocolates, tins of cashews
his doctor advised him to avoid.

Temptations he could not refuse.
Foibles his loved ones once enjoyed,

still amusing, if unwise,
piled curbside with last week's news.

Home and Away

My father stood on a stage
at the far end of the firehouse hall,
townspeople muttering
as he spoke in the same tone
he used one night as I turned in,
suggesting I take an outside pitch
to the opposite field. *Don't try to pull,*

he said, *You won't get around on it.*
Now he advised our neighbors
to accept the busing of city kids
to our schools north of the city.
It was 1964, and he was not really
discussing geography, and I never
forgot how he did not raise his voice

as they raised theirs. He did not get
red in the face or clench his jaw.
He just took their high hard one
and lined it to right field, smiling,
a clever batsman for the home team.
That fall, as ball season wound down,
the children arrived, my classmates

at first calling them *the dark kids*,
but soon they acquired real names
and were called to lead the Pledge,
to take the count for hot or cold
lunch, to pass out the lined paper,
to sky on the playground swings,
to round the sandy uncut diamond.

Acknowledgements

I am grateful for the support and encouragement I have received from many people, including fellow poets and writers James Cole, Philip Done, John Guzlowski, John Jeffire, Judith Kerman, John Palen, Skip Renker, Michael Somers, JodiAnn Stevenson, Jeff Vande Zande, and Adrienne Wright.

Thanks also to Midland, Michigan's Herbert H. Dow Gardens, Creative 360, the Live Oaks Cafe, and Saginaw, Michigan's Theodore Roethke Home and Museum for providing opportunities for public readings.

I am also grateful to *Third Wednesday,* where several of the poems in this book first appeared, and to Nick Courtright of Atmosphere Press for his astute and gracious editorial guidance, and for allowing this book to see the light of day.

Special thanks to Rob Hyner of Avon CT, photographer and friend, for use of his photo for the front and back cover of this book.

About Atmosphere Press

Atmosphere Press is an independent full-service publisher for books in genres ranging from non-fiction to fiction to poetry, with a special emphasis on being an author-friendly approach to getting a book into the world. Learn more about what we do at Atmosphere's website, atmospherepress.com.

And of course, we encourage you to check out some of Atmosphere's latest releases, which are available at Amazon.com, BarnesandNoble.com, and via order from your local bookstore:

Ghost Sentence, poems by Mary Flanagan

What Outlives Us, poems by Larry Levy

Bello the Cello, a children's book by Dennis Mathew

That Beautiful Season, a novel by Sandra Fox Murphy

What I Cannot Abandon, poems by William Guest

Such a Nice Girl, a novel by Carol St. John

All the Dead Are Holy, poems by Larry Levy

How Not to Sell, nonfiction by Rashad Daoudi

Rescripting the Workplace, nonfiction by Pam Boyd

Surviving Mother, a novella by Gwen Head

Winter Park, a novel by Graham Guest

About the Author

Larry Levy's previous collections of poetry include *I Would Stay Forever If I Could and New Poems* (Mayapple Press) and *All the Dead are Holy* (Atmosphere Press).

His poems have appeared in *The Virginia Quarterly Review, The Driftwood Review, Third Wednesday, South Carolina Review, Controlled Burn,* and other little and online magazines. For several years he has served as judge for *Third Wednesday's* annual poetry contest.

Retired from teaching at every level from pre-school to graduate school, Larry and his wife Cheryl live in Midland, Michigan where they direct plays and musicals for the Midland Center for the Arts youth theater.

9 781642 049145